The Call
Of The Phoenix -
Vignettes Of Old And
New China

Our home in Beijing

The Call
Of The Phoenix -
Vignettes Of Old
And New China

by Robert M. Bartlett

Illustrations by Jan Norton

Peter E. Randall
PUBLISHER

Peter E. Randall Publisher
Box 4726, Portsmouth, NH 03801

**Library of Congress Cataloging-in-Publication
Data**

Bartlett, Robert M.,
        The call of the phoenix

        1. China--Poetry. 2. Revolutionists--China--
Interviews.   I. Title
PS3552.A7659C3 1987 811' .54   87-9514
ISBN 0-914339-19-2

To
Su Chen (Sue Nuckols Bartlett)
who shared with me the adventurous years
at Yenching University
in Beijing
and my continuing study of China

Other Books by Robert M. Bartlett

My Corner of New England
The Faith of the Pilgrims
The Pilgrim Way
Thanksgiving Day
They Stand Invincible -- Men Who Are Reshaping
      Our World
Sky Pioneer -- The Story of Igor I. Sikorsky
They Dared to Live
They Dared to Believe
The Great Empire of Silence
Pilgrim House by the Sea

天下一家

UNDER HEAVEN ONE FAMILY

(from the *Book of Rites*)

Contents

Part II - My Visits with Chinese Revolutionaries

Part III - New China

Foreword

IN 1924 WHEN I HAD FINISHED my graduate work at Yale University I went to Beijing to teach Western literature at Yenching University. The place was vibrating with the Chinese Renaissance. There was a brain trust of reformers centered at the National University. It was my privilege to meet and visit with many of these men and write about them for American papers and magazines.

My admiration for the Chinese people and my study of their unfinished revolution have continued through the years.

This book is arranged in three sections. Part I, Old China, is a series of poems that give insight into the vitality and color of Chinese life before the rule of Mao Tzdong. Part II contains my visits with major Chinese revolutionaries. Part III, New China, is a collection of poems and sketches that reveal some of the changes under the Communist regime. They remind us of the complexity of the revolution and the fact that the majority of the foremost leaders were not Communists.

Photographs taken by the author sixty years ago in China were used as reference by the artist in drawing the pen and ink sketches which illustrate this book. The sketch of the phoenix which appears on the cover and on the title page was drawn from a stone engraving dating from the Han dynesty.

The title, *The Call of the Phoenix - Vignettes of Old and New China*, comes from Chinese mythology. Tradition tells that this bird, *feng huang*, appears only when reason prevails in the country. Its coming heralds a new period of tranquility and progress.

13

Acknowledgments

I WISH TO THANK Mr. C. Y. Hsu, my brilliant student at Yenching University, Beijing, a scholar of Chinese and Occidental cultures, for researching the history of the phoenix and writing the Chinese calligraphy.

The Christian Science Monitor published many of the poems in the book and *Current History* published my first interviews with Chinese revolutionists. The Library of Congress provided some of the photographs of the revolutionaries.

I thank Dr. Eugene Wu of the Harvard-Yenching Library for his many courtesies, Academia Sinica, Dr. Harold Worthley, Congregational Library, Boston, Plymouth Public Library, Collier County and University of Miami libraries.

I am grateful to Lois Hanggi, my faithful and gifted typist.

Quotations have been made from the following authors and titles: George Poloczi Horvath, *Emperor of the Blue Ants,* Doubleday, New York, 1963; Roderick MacFarquar, *Chairman Mao - Politics Take Command,* Massachusetts Institute of Technology, Cambridge, 1966; George Urban, *The Miracles of Chairman Mao,* Tom Stacey, London, 1971; Simon Leys, *Peking Shadows,* Viking Press, New York, 1977; Jonathan D. Spence, *The Gate of Heavenly Peace,* Viking Press, New York, 1981, page 207; from Liang Qichao, *Nianpu* page 727; Lyon Sharman, *Sun Yatsen, His Life and Its Meaning,* John Day, New York, 1932; and Orville Shell, *To Get Rich is Glorious, China in the 1980s,* Pantheon, New York, 1984; Harrison Salisbury, *The Long March,* Harper & Row, New York, 1985.

15

Part I
Old China

Beijing Pigeons

From city gates and temple eaves
The silver squadrons launch
Into the evening light,
In swift maneuvers wing
A flashing cruise.

With organ trills they play
A swooping scale
And brighten dingy city streets
With wings that beat a mellow
Note of cheer into the air.

Swift whistling tones,
Carillons of sweet melody,
Bold dashing messengers
From walls and towers fling out
A bell-like call to prayer.

In currents of mad ecstasy,
In pure wild gladness wheel
A hundred whirling circles over man,
And speed a white breath
From cloudland's purity.

(The famous Beijing pigeons with bamboo whistles attached to
their wings were eliminated by the Communists along with
their "kill the sparrows" crusade.)

The Streets Of Beijing

The streets and boulevards of Beijing
Teemed with sights and smells
And rumble of pulsating multitudes.
We maneuvered on our bicycles cautiously
Alert to congestion and noise and wailing
Beggars with outstretched hands.
We dodged the fertilizer guild coolies
With their wheelbarrows of nightsoil.

A farmer was driving a white pig to
The butcher,
Tapping it with a long willow stick.
A shepherd boy herded five bewildered sheep
To market, their woolly backs
Splattered with red paint.
Before an open blacksmith shop
A recalcitrant horse was being shod.
Against the wall a porcelain mender plied
His craft with consummate
Skill. A barber carried
On his trade nearby. He soaked
The whiskered face
With foamy water from the brass bowl.
Finishing his shave, he cleaned out
The ears of his
Smiling client, then shouldered his
Equipment on a bamboo pole and, twanging
His jews-harp, trudged
On his daily rounds.

The knife sharpener blew a shrill
Brass trumpet.

A clicking wooden castanet was the sign
Of the pedicure.
Open shops sold meat dumplings, pork,
Chicken and rabbit. Shoppers rested
On benches, sipping steaming hot tea in cups
Without handles, watching the pipe mender
Insert bamboo stems into metal bowls,
Readying them to cheer some weary coolie
Who would pause for a smoke.

All this servicing of the people
Took place in a pandemonium of traffic.
There were fleets of rickshaws pulled
By human beings.
They formed a clamorous throng with the
Challenging cry of the
Pullers, *chieh gwang, chieh gwang,*
(Borrow my shadow or get out of my way).

Long carts of heavy beams were pulled by
Half a dozen coolies and in and out wove
A horse carriage with shining brass
Lamps and musical gongs.
Marriage processions
Were common with the red decorated
Palinquins carrying the bride
To the home of the groom.

Funeral corteges
Passed, the bearers in white
For mourning, reminders of life and
Death, in the pressure of
Daily living.*

*To alter the spelling of a venerable name like Peking requires compromise. But this is the ruling of the new *Pinyin* system that Peking shall now be Beijing along with changes in names of many places and people.

Persimmons

Before the coming of the snow,
when heavy frosts on tile roofs glow,
My vender brings new goods to show
"S-h-i-h-tzu! Mei s-h-i-h-tzu!"

In long and tattered sheep-skin coat
He leans to make his chanting float
Above the tower and palace moat
"S-h-i-h-tzu! Mei s-h-i-h-tzu!"

With baskets spread beside the wall,
The mellow, golden fruit of fall
Makes proof of this cheery call,
"S-h-i-h-tzu! Mei s-h-i-h-tzu!"

With early evening's shadows gray
He swings his saffron fruit, with gay
Shrill chant, and wanders far away
"S-h-i-h-tzu! Mei s-h-i-h-tzu!"

(In Mandarin "S-h-i-h-tzu! Mei s-h-i-h-tzu!" means
"Persimmons! Buy persimmons!")

Bridgeway Of The Past

A camel's back of marble stairs
Arches the slender Brook of Jade
Where runs the Green Pagoda spring
Along white sands. Here pheasant
And the mottled deer drank in the early
Dawn and scampered when the yellow
Robed courtiers of the palace
Knelt and prayed to heaven.

Grass crowds the imperial way, grows
On the stairs,
And high weeds choke the path of princes.
Gray squares of time-worn stone change
Into softened gold as the
Shade of willow boughs
Shifts in the evening light; and phantom
Shadows form beside the ancient balustrade
And walk again upon the regal bridge,
A procession from the long forgotten past.

The Temple
Of The Silent Oak

The temple moonlight sends a scare of shadows
Here and there, while bamboo hang
In silvery sheaths
And shake against the wall.
The stream in sparkling channels leaps
Down terraced ways to feed the
Silent, crouching lions,
Whose cold watchfulness keeps guard
Against intrusions from the mountain pass.

Below the oak, white patches, slim islands
In a sea of night, dance recklessly.
Gold tendrils from the moon
Cling to the unlit rooms,
Homes of the pallid gods that stare in sleep.
The golden shafts trip to the battered doors,
Play at the window squares, but go not in.
These stolid gods crouch musty black
Under their bejewelled roofs, dumb
To the light-fancies of the sky.

Sacred Lotus
At The Summer Palace

Slick glistening leaves ride
The slow undulation of the pond,
Dip their cool edges in the
Jade brook's green,
Rise to embrace buds of coral pink
And sink again where the clustering pines
Throw shadows from the hill.

Below the ornate balustrade curling pads
Lap with gentle lift and fall.
The carved stone walls are jutting
Fortresses that mingle with the roots and moss
In the deep mirrowed castle towers.

Within the marble borders of the lake
Pink gems float in fair colonies,
A multitude of scents that wake
Each day with new perfume,
The ancient lotus flowers
That grace the palace of a queen.

The Water Vender

With fading stars and early hours
The plodding whine will come,
The squeaking, jarring discord
Of the water vender's cart,
A mossy, shining surface
With a sharp complaining cry.

When ice holds on the sprocket,
On the hub and handle bars,
Encasing every spirit with its chill,
The slowly moving groaner
Wheels in shrieks of agony.

Gobi dust blows up the roadway,
Draping roofs in somber cloud,
Blinding, chokes up every creature
Save this shrill, defiant note.
With rainy torrents falling,
Muddy gutters stormed and full,
The unconquered plows each puddle
Creaking in bespattered treble.

The blatant, jarring cacophony
Of the water vender's cart
On methodic changeless circuit,
With its ache-complaining cry,
Tempts quiet stars to frowning
In the sleepy hours of dawn.

Camels At A Well

In torrid summer the furry cavalcade
Will halt, while drivers tug and lift
The bulging sacks of lime and coal.
The camels shrug the dust from their gaunt humps
And plant their padded feet
For a siesta by the wall.

Where date trees shade the road,
Beside the gold-tiled Beijing tower,
They drink from a rough tub
As coolies splash the brimming pails
Brought by a long pole sweep
From the stone depths.

While resting on the dusty path
They lie head to tail, in line,
Bound by their marching ropes.
These inseparable companions of the caravan
Crunch lean yellow jaws
And shut their sun-red eyes.

With grumbled remonstrance they assume
Their heavy packs and swing
Along the gray city wall
In rhythmic monotony, pat-pat-pat,
And fade like brown threads
Along the far off roads.

A Poignant Memory

My first rickshaw ride was in Shanghai in 1924.
　　Soon after landing from the *S.S. Cleveland*
Sue and I were venturing forth to dine
　　At the Astor Hotel. It was humiliating to climb
Into that vehicle and look down on the runner
　　Who was about the age of my father but only
Half his size. He wore nothing except thong
　　Sandals and coolie cloth breeches. Sue's
Puller was even smaller and more wizened than
　　mine.

We rolled out onto the avenue
　　To join a stream of rickshaws, hand carts,
Wheelbarrows and swarms of laborers on foot
　　Bearing bags of cement, grain and farm produce,
Crates and boxes. It was a dizzying
　　Introduction into the coolie world where
Burdens were heavy and human life cheap.

At the Astor we had just alighted from our
　　Carriages and were standing on the sidewalk
When a chauffeur-driven car moved in
　　Behind us. A pompous white man jumped out,
Banging his door, and delivered a vicious kick
　　At the rear of my rickshaw, shouting,
"Get out of my way, you Chink!" With that
He berated my runner, who cringed and hurriedly

Pulled away. The Chinese doorman
   In red and gold uniform,
Ignoring the indignity, calmly ushered us
   Into the Victorian lobby.

Chrysanthemums

Tier after tier of clustering heads,
Bronze, golden, yellow, crimson-tipped,
A mass of haunting shades, the piled up
Gems of old Cathay, live on,
A hundred colored filaments, the touch
Of garnet, mulberry, amethyst, skill of
Gardeners from past centuries,
Multitudinous tints of the immortal flower.

They wake with autumn winds
In season with a riot of coloring,
And when the last of sailing leaves
Drift to the palace walls, they stand
Green and assured within the courtyards
Of monarchs gone, indomitable.

(After the Beijing Chrysanthemum Show)

Night Fall On Chihli Bay

The fishing boats along the Chinese sand
    Loom black against the coral sky
Like stranded deep sea monsters cast on land
    With gaunt, worn claws and feelers lifted high.

The shallow pools left by the evening tide
    Reflect small fragments of the pink and gold
From fading clouds and form a magic, wide
    Expanse of scattered jewels about the hold

Of each dark junk. Boatmen chant their call
    And spread their nets across the darkening bay
That reaches its still silver to the tall
    Stone passes of Tung Yu Shan's rock-bound way.

The last reflections, covered by hovering cloud,
    Soon fade into blurred grayness while the light
Of the contending moon casts her dim shroud
    On boats and shore and closes all in night.

A New Friend

I walked along the *hutung* one bright morning
    Between gray brick walls and painted
Doorways, most of which were closed and
    The inner courtyards quiet.
I passed a faded red door that was half open.
    A small lad stood on the granite step.
He was about four years of age and
    Dressed in blue pants and a bright red
Jacket. His thick black hair looked as if
    It had been cut under an inverted
Rice bowl. In the quiet moments
    Of the day's awakening he seemed to be
Half dreaming, clutching a stuffed
    Pekinese dog in his hands.

He did not glance my way until I stooped
    To greet him, "*Nin hao, hsao p'engyo*"
(How are you, little friend), I said.
    His slanted eyes widened. His lips
Trembled and he closed his arms
    Protectingly about his dog. I spoke
To him gently, but he turned abruptly
    And sped over the brick squares of the
Courtyard and disappeared.

What could have frightened him, I thought as
    I moved along. It must have been
My appearance, a foreigner
    In his neighborhood. Possibly he had
Never seen a westerner before. I was
    Taller than the average Chinese, with
A mop of shaggy light brown hair, pale skin,
    Bushy eyebrows and a prominent
Roman nose. Maybe I looked
    Like a "foreign devil."

For some time I kept watch for
    My little friend.
I was cautious in passing his house.
    One day I saw him standing just inside
The big wooden door, peering out. He bobbed
    Back out of view
But without his original panic.
    I called to him softly saying that I was
His new friend.
    He did not answer me. On a later encounter
He was riding his toy Mongolian pony, its
    Head painted red and blue and
Mounted on a long stick. He moved closer.
    I bent over to inspect his
Cherished possession and said,
    "*How kan*" (Pretty). He lightened up
And offered his pony to me.

It was a bridge-building gesture made to
The mysterious outsider
    Who had come to live nearby.
"Thank you," I replied, "I like your pony."
    He smiled happily as if a burden had rolled
Off his mind, his big brown eyes accepting me.
    "Beautiful," I said and
I passed the pony back to him.
    He held it close. He was pleased
With the bridge he had built
    Between himself and a stranger.

Tan Cheh Ssu

(A Buddhist Monastery)

Through terraced courts, up winding steps of stone
I've climbed, to see below, time-scarred and old,
The yellow roofs ascend like stairs of gold
And in and out as ghosts of spirits flown
Move priests who in low chanting monotone
Call men to prayer; wisteria blooms unfold
From temple eaves. There bowed before the cold
Proud gods, monks make their gifts to the unknown.

The majesty of years. Wide reach of days.
In quiet exultation comes an end
To my vain questionings for here our ways
Converge. The differences grow dim. Thoughts blend
And make of all aims one, one as the rays
Of light, as distances, one with the wind.

White Swans
In November

Upon the ice-edged garden lake
A royal navy drifts in sail,
And caught by light and rippling breeze
Is pushed into a weedy maze.
November twilight drops a pale
Of yellow in the liquid green to play
A fairy shadow game in rings
Of emerald, scattered jewels afloat
To deck the silken, snow-white wings.

The marble bridgeway casts aslant
Weird shadows where carved barges clung
Beside the phoenix-dragon slab.
Here gold-brown leaves wash into shoals
And naked willow boughs are hung.
The silent, groping chill
Is pierced; keen as a knife the cry
From out the necks of lifted pride
Is flung -- defiance to the sky.

(A view from our courtyard.)

41

The Poet in Old China

The poet has been an esteemed dignitary in
    Old China. He was a master of the mysterious
Characters that compose the classical language.
    He arranged them in a fashion that spoke
To the soul of the people.

The highest honor to come to a magistrate
    Was to create with his writing brush an
        affirmation
Of truth that would be read and honored
    For generations. The poem was the noblest
Form of the written language. It could live
    Forever.

Poets were favorite subjects of the artists,
    Who drew them, brush in hand, contemplating
The order of nature or framing in illustrious
    Words the virtues and values of human life.
Ch'u Yuan, as Dante in Italy and Milton in
    England, inspired a succession of poets
Like Li Po and Tu Fu, who established the
    Fame of the poet in Chinese culture.

The Candy Man

Outside the gateway of the frozen street
The old man jingles his brass gongs,
A ceaseless "tinkle, tinkle, c-l-a-n-g!"
He kicks his feet against the wall,
Tugs his blue cotton cloak about him
And calls, "Here every sweet I sell!"

With evening he will push his loaded cart
Below my wall, light his oil lamp,
Arrange his baskets of chestnuts, red haws and
Candied things, and call a piercing drawn-out
"Come! Every sweet to buy!"
With a "tinkle, tinkle, c-l-a-n-g!"

Dust clouds whip down the narrow *hutung*
And spread their gray chill
Through walled-in courts;
The trot of ricksha men, a carriage gong
And then the dauntless man sings out
His cheery "Sweets! Sweets! Come and buy!"
And his gongs jingle "tinkle, tinkle, c-l-a-n-g!"

The Charcoal Peddler

Always bringing charcoal from the country past
The fill
Where aged oak trees fringe the hill.
He cut and burned the logs along the river wide,
Woodcocks watching at his side.

When the snow falls he will come
With beating on his drum,
Broken covered baskets swinging into place
And a sooty, streaked face
On turning back to town.

Mystery in his manner and richness in his call,
In the wild from spring to fall,
He knows the forest trees and creatures
Through his long and lonely hours
Before turning back to town.

Bowls Of Millet

I meet them on parade day after day,
As I walk to early morning classes,
The little waifs with mangy heads and
Pinched faces smeared with grime, wrapped
In their cotton coats. Mothers trudge
With babies on their backs. Old men, bent
Over, plod. They wear ear-flaps and rags
Tied about their heads.
Women stumble on bound feet
And lean on crooked sticks.
Dust whips at the wall and leaves
Their hungry visages gray-caked.

All winter with the zero dawn, they creep
From all around for a bowl
Of steamed grain.
By eight o'clock this cortège of the poor
Lines the old Manchu villa wall.
They cringe beside its giant gate,
Like starving scarecrows in the wind.
The famished multitude wait
For their portion of millet
And cling to life for one more day.

(A private service project carried on near the Yenching
University campus.)

46

Gold Garden

A colony of suns, the yellow spheres
Of full unfurled chrysanthemums
Crowd the pathways by the flags
Of dusty stone. Above dark leaves
Soft petals curl their folded grace
In feathery balls. Tall clustered marigolds
Hold their amber crests up to the sun
And wave with each October breeze
Within a sea of sunny gold.

The canary tints of zinnias tower
Above nasturtiums, whose peeping orange buds
Mark the ambitious climb to reach the cerise
Of ivy vines upon the wall.
Those bobbing heads of sunshine bend
As topaz fragments from the dates sail down
To mix in the golden carpet of the fall.

(Our own autumn flowers)

The Castaway

One April day I walked alone beside the city wall
For spring had come.
I met an old and toothless wraith.
It carried on its back a hump of rags.
It stopped and feebly tied a wisp of cabbage
With a string. And then it moved along
With swaying, aimless trudge,
And hopeless stare. Made in God's image?
A trash picker with peach blossoms in her hair.

Evening Bell

All bird calls fell; the breeze stopped playing
    With the slim date leaves and sunset threw
A purple quiet upon the hills; long pack trains
    Stood beside the trails, still silhouettes,
To wait that ringing bell.

Gaunt, blown pines waved shoots of faith
    Above the courts and let their softening
Shadows fall upon the shaded tints of roofs that
    Seemed to bear light magic touches from
The clouds when the bell boomed thunderingly.

Priests flickered in the dim court yards and stole
    Into the sanctuary and in kneeling prayer
Joined mystically with chanted cry unto the night,
    A guttural monotone of petitions to Buddha,
Led by the beaten rumble of the bell.

To A Young Soldier
Killed By Looting Troops

His cotton coat is stiffened with
A clotted bloody stain.
The young face has known too soon the
Bitterness of pain.
By the temple wall he lies while the
Pigeons fly again,
Their whistles sounding the melodious
Refrain.

He had caught them in his boyhood, fixed
The music to their wings
And stroked their gleaming feathers grown
In newness of the spring.
He had lived in play and study, tasting all
The wholesome joys
And now they rob the village of its
Priceless treasure, boys!

They lay dying, piled up moaning beside
The western gate
While the marauding soldiers wreaked their
Vengeance and their hate;
The threatened girls and mothers cringed
Fearful of their fate.

Old men recounted the terrors in the time
Of some past reign,
Children saw war's curses and interest
Seemed to feign,
Soon to forget its blinded folly, its
Horror, wrong and pain,
To join in scattering life upon the
City's plain.

The doves were driven from the temple by
The crows that came to glean
And kind night settled with them over
Man's constant passion scene.

(When war lords were contending for rule of Beijing.)

The Chinese New Year

To walk with the surging crowd at the
    New Year Fair brings a breath of freedom.
The jostling throngs break ties with
    Burdens and cares of life. There is
Liberation in the first hours of the
    New season. People free their minds of
Mistakes made and debts unpaid. They walk
    Now in rhythm with a new vista.
The elation is contagious.

Fluttering banners lift spirits and posters
    Spell out health, prosperity and
Happiness. The calls of peddlers and
    Shop keepers are music to the ears. The
Sunny winter air offers release
    From chilled dwellings.
People feast their eyes on booths of
    Fireworks and enjoy the crackle and bang
Of noisy attacks against evil spirits.

One can buy winter comforts like padded
    Pants and jackets, knitted caps, gloves
And cloth boots lined with sheep's wool.
    Carts are loaded with toys - horses,
Wagons, home made dolls, cloth animals,
    Windmills and bright colored balls.

Candy salesmen dust their wares
　　With chicken feathers tied to
A long stick - chocolate squares,
　　Candied fruits and enticing morsels
Of gold, red and green.

Trained monkeys, dogs and white mice
　　Perform. The air is full of the happy
Squeals of children. Shops on wheels
　　Display apples, persimmons, pears,
Bread, dumplings, cakes, caldrons
　　Of hot soup and pots
Of steaming tea that help one forget
　　The days of hunger.
The celebrants count their
　　Coppers and indulge themselves in
The luxuries spread before them.
　　Visions of brighter days dance
In their heads. It is time to rest
　　A measure and to look forward.
The Year of the Dog is ending
　　And the Year of the Dragon is dawning.

Turnips

White turnips beside the littered
    Shack where six coolies come
At night to huddle on the cold clay floor
    For rest. Here at the morning and the evening
Meal they crouch about a smouldering fire
    Of weeds and sticks, from the mean winds,
And talk of carts, of sawing logs and
    Dragging heavy things. After hot water,
Without tea, they may have corn meal cakes
    And turnips or some cabbage leaves.

Then one small bowl from a long-stemmed
    Pipe -- a dozen puffs, and sleep.
Day after day the turnip pile
    Beside the door grows smaller and then
The hard white roots are put in brine,
    And in the bitter winter time the luxury
Of salty pickles with bread cakes,
    Green leaves and hot water will cheer
The dark and fireless hut of
    China's burden bearers.

A Late Summer Storm

With the timid flame of my candle light
I keep guard through the black and mourning night
In Nan T'ai Ho, beside the pane
Of a tiny window, as swirling rain
Encloses the crumbling Chinese wall.
The glow from my candle is lost in the fall
Of rain on the sodden street
And quivers when the north winds beat
With a weird unceasing moan on the low
And sprawling dwellings of Nan T'ai Ho.

The fishing junks along the beach
Are driven to the shore, where the screech
Of weary birds protests in the face
Of storm; and the cold and weeping base
Of Mount lu Shan beats off the foam
Of angry waves from its rocky home.
But the candle gleam in the miry road
Sends, in tremulous glint, a cheerful code
That spells peace and tomorrow's sunset glow,
Which will come to storm-swept Nan T'ai Ho.

(Written on the coast of Chirli Bay in North China, summer of
1926.)

Carry The Ox Mountain

Carry the Ox Mountain is a small peak
    In the rugged country along Chihli Bay.
A legendary prince of this hill kingdom
    Received a warning that barbarians from the
North were marching toward his peaceful land.
    In desperation the prince knelt before
The jade Buddha in his palace. As he
    Prayed for guidance, a voice spoke to him:
"Take a black ox from your herd
    And carry it to the top of the highest peak
In your realm. Then Heaven may grant your
    People protection."

The prince made his way in a blinding rain
    Storm through dense thickets to the rocky
Trail that led to the long and treacherous
    Incline to the summit, bearing the ox on
His back. There he prayed to Buddha to
    Save his people. The invading horde spared
His province.

A shrine was erected on Carry the Ox Mountain
    To commemorate the devotion of the prince.
When I was there a Buddhist priest was
    Maintaining the memorial. He lived in a
Crude cottage surrounded by his vegetable
    Garden and a pile of twigs and branches
For his cooking. Near the entrance to the
    Shrine was a large iron bell suspended
Between two lichen-covered slabs
    Of stone. The genial monk in blue cotton
Robe and round black hat moved about with the

Measured composure of one who had tasted
The bliss of Nirvana
    During his hours of solitude.
Deep brown eyes looked out on
    His chosen realm of quiet with contentment.

He had found all the wisdom he needed in
    Buddha and Confucius. These two
Contemporaries were his teachers.
    Historically the followers
Of Confucius accepted Buddhist disciples.
    Both religions were less aggressive
Than Christians and Moslems and willing
    To tolerate one another.

The monk on top of Carry the Ox Mountain
    was not conscious of all the
Profound insights of these two holy men
    Of Asia. But he loved
The call to prayer when the temple bell
    Boomed forth. He loved
The chants from the sacred books
    That linked him with
The timeless and eternal.

(I took a photograph of him and his bell, which the artist has
drawn here.)

Chinese Kites

They cover the shop front,
Gay butterflies, green dragons,
Fish, tiger heads, sea gulls,
Scarlet hawks and giant owls.
The crowding lookers watch
The moving tissue on the wall.
Children test with grimy hands
The thickness of the paper wings,
And laugh in wiggling joy.

When coppers can be found to buy
Down narrow lanes they will run
And fly their parchment treasures
High over towers, moats
And palace walls.
The air will soon be singing
With the wind on whipping cord,
And these bright-colored fantasies
Will dive and soar above
The dusty city streets
And welcome in the coming
Of the spring.

The Gateman
And His Pet Lark

Our modest Chinese house was located
    Along with other faculty homes, in
The Garden of Moonlight Fertility. Our
    Watchman occupied the brick gate house
At the entrance. He lived alone with his lark
    Which had a speckled breast and a
Lyric voice. The lark was his pride and joy.

Gateman Fu walked about the
    Garden and village streets with his
Feathered friend in a cage or fettered
    On an open perch. Strolling with one's
Bird was a cherished custom in Old China.
    On mild days one often saw
These sedate bird walkers on their promenades.

Fu spent most of his daytime hours
    On a wooden bench beside his front window
With the lark's cage hanging
    From a hook under the eaves of his house.
The cage was covered with a
    Hood when weather was cool, otherwise
Open to the sun.

The nut brown bird poured out
    Accolades of praise for the gift of the day
While Fu smoked his long black
    Stemmed pipe. The tea kettle steamed
Away on the brick stove. His cup
    Was beside him. Drying tea leaves
Fluttered on the window sill. They were
    Used over and over again.

Our border collie was often
    There beside his two friends. Scottie
Had taken over control of the Garden.
    Morning and evening he made his rounds.
He was always ready for a walk
    With Fu and the lark.

The little gateman in blue coolie cloth,
    The lark and the border collie
Shared adventures in contentment.
    I can still hear the sweet voiced singer
Delivering a vesper hymn
    To the setting sun
With Fu and Scottie sharing
    This paean of praise.

(Yenching University had purchased an old Manchu estate
called the Garden of Moonlight Fertility and renovated and
remodeled some of the buildings for faculty residences.)

The Coal Coolie

Pushing, straining,
Crouched beneath his harness,
Grimy pads upon his shoulders,
Hands that grip the cold, slick wood,
Worn by days of toiling.

Shouting, calling
For each frequent corner,
Turning now to twist and wind
Patiently up each incline
Through the noisy alley.

Resting, smoking
The long bowl pipe
Just as used and broken,
While coal-streaked mouth and eyes
Grin on life's illusion.

Bending, lifting
As the wheel turns up around
Tiny bells will tinkle out.
Does he follow each big circuit,
Feast upon its cheery sound?

(We bought coal from him for our kitchen stove.)

Lantern Festival

Along the narrow village street,
With its mud walls and gray-tile roofs,
Are hung the swinging globes of light,
Glazed balls of green, of blue and red,
A fairyland of sparkling tints
Swinging in the summer night.

These glowing pendants in far groves
Of deep and shadowed pine send out
Across the darkened hill rays
Of color to the White Cloud Pagoda,
Glowing ruby, emerald, gold
Swaying up the terraced ways.

I climb the gay-hung lantern trail
Between the spheres of tinted silk
Into the cool of white pine glades
And see below a jewelled land.
The wakened countryside is caught
In the rhythm of softened shades
Gleaming in this Festival of Lights.

A Gentleman
Of Old Beijing

Dong! Dong! A padded shoe stamps on the bell;
He tugs the fur robe to his chest,
Snugs his long-nailed fingers into capacious
Sleeves. The cigarette from a carved ivory holder
Trails a haze about his deep and fatty eyes.
With pompous dignity he fills the sleek, black robe,
Complacent and separate in silk and fur.

With sleepy indolence he rides
Above the rickshaw runner -- a sweating slave
Without the pale of his gentility.
Down broad streets he rolls with inflated
Effort to be seen a gentleman.
And through the noisy alleys he clangs his gong
And curses in his languid pride
At beggars and the dirty mob of lower men.

Part II
My Visits With Major Chinese Revolutionists

Sun Yatsen and his wife, Ching Ling

Sun Yatsen
Father of the Revolution

THE SWEEP OF CHINA'S revolution is too much for the western mind to sort out and comprehend. It reaches back to the time when the Middle Kingdom was an isolated realm of Manchu despotism and anti-westernism. These trubulent days remind us of the Opium Wars and other military moves to force China to do business with the West. After the defeat of the Boxer Uprising, gunboat diplomacy and exploitation of extraterritorial rights led to years of anti-foreign demonstrations.

Japan's arch blunder, the invasion of China in 1937, exhausted China's resources and killed millions of people. The eight year holocaust so devastated the country that Mao Tzdong was able to engulf the people in his proletariat revolution. He had forced Chiang Kaishek to carry the burden of defense against Japan while he built up his anti-government forces in Yanan. Japan had laid the groundwork for Mao to take over.

Communist doctrine has ruled since 1949. Western observers, glancing at the complexity of the revolution may assume that the Maoist regime has been the primary builder of the New China, which is a gross misunderstanding.

In this section I present brief sketches of some of the noteworthy reformers who made lasting contributions to China's progress. Their names have not been promoted by Party propaganda although they have been major forces in China's revolution.

Sun Yatsen was one of the many Christian Chinese who sacrificed his life for liberation along with Confucianists, Buddhists, agnostics and atheists.

For years I had looked forward to the day when I could meet Sun Yatsen, the father of New China. I had read about his quest for freedom. One day he was a refugee in the British Embassy in London with Manchu spies demanding his arrest. Then he appeared in South Asia, in Hawaii and in Japan. He was always pursued by Ching dynasty supporters and Chinese vested interests, who forced him to live in exile.

This life-long peripatetic for freedom arrived in Beijing from Nanjing in the winter of 1925. Through frustrating years his plans for a New China had not been given a chance.

Discouraged by the mountainous obstacles that blocked the progress of his republic, Sun had sighed, "My people are a rope of sand." An amalgam of ignorance and lethargy, they could not form a movement strong enough to hold them together. Who could cope with 400,000,000 people, shackled by illiteracy, poverty, without inter-communication, and devoid of national will!

Following the Revolution of 1911 a council was called of all the provinces that had declared their independence. On December 29 this body met and without waiting for negotiations with the north, they elected Sun Yatsen provisional president. January 1, 1912 he was inaugurated. But Beijing people rejected him because he was a Cantonese, lacked experience in government and was considered too radical.

Although the republic had a president in name the Empress Dowager was still on the throne. Yuan Shikai urged Sun to resign, stating that he himself would act as premier and see that the empire became a republic. Sun resigned in good faith. But there was wide-spread disagreement throughout the country. The Nanjing group endeavored to oust Yuan in the Second Revolution which led to increased bitterness and civil strife.

By 1915 Yuan Shikai had become president and Sun Yatsen's Guomindang members had been pushed out of the government in Beijing. Yuan's assumption of power was opposed by Sun.

Yuan died June 6, 1916. Sun returned from Japan, where he had been in exile, to lead the cause of republican government through his lecturing and writing.

Michael Borodin arrived in China in 1923 posing as a press correspondent. He came to serve as an adviser to Sun and to promote the Chinese Communist Party. The Soviet missionary exerted considerable influence on some Guomindang members.

General Chiang Kaishek balked at carrying out orders from Stalin and severed relations with the U.S.S.R. Borodin was told to pack up and go home. However, he left a nucleus of Leninites who eventually bourgeoned forth into a monolithic control over the Middle Kingdom.

Dr. Sun's desperate need for foreign aid, denied him by western powers, had encouraged him to accept Lenin's offer to help. In the spring of 1923 Sun sent Chiang Kaishek to Russia to size up the Communists. Lenin was critically ill but Chiang talked with many Party leaders. Chiang was conscious of the divisions and strife in the Party.

He pointed out flaws in the system and said the Russians did not understand the Chinese.

"They insisted on dividing China into classes and advocated struggle between them. I was profoundly disappointed," Chiang emphasized.

After three months in the U.S.S.R. Chiang wrote: "I became more and more convinced that Soviet political institutions were instruments of tyranny and terror and basically incompatible with the principles of the Guomindang."[*]

In the midst of all this turmoil Sun remained the symbol against Manchu tyranny. He was the rallying point for reform. He was the oracle speaking eloquently to his people up to the day of his death.

Weakened by interminable years of anxiety and hardship, he was operated on for cancer at Beijing Union Medical College. He died January 26, 1925 in the home of Wellington Koo. He had said to his brother-in-law, Dr. H. H. Kung, "We are Christians. I would like a Christian funeral." A memorial service was held in the chapel of Beijing Union Medical College.

The casket of the reformer was placed temporarily in the Buddhist temple of Pi Yun Ssu, the Temple of the Azure Clouds, in the Western Hills outside Beijing. The peace of this shrine offered a resting place for the crusader who said, "I am a coolie and the son of a coolie and I will always work for the masses."

As a teen-ager, Sun had given a fiery speech against idolatry in his local temple, snatching off a finger from one of the images. The village elders

---

[*] Chiang Kaishek

suggested exile and the lad was sent to Hong Kong. He was befriended there by missionaries and became a Christian and graduated from medical school.

The weak governments in Nanjing and Beijing were unable to memorialize the reformer who laid out a new path for the country with his Three Peopleism program - *San Min Chu-i*. The three principles were: (1) Overthrow of the Manchu dynasty and restoration of the Chinese as rulers of their nation, (2) Constitutional government, (3) Livelihood of the people based on Christian and Socialist concepts.

I wanted to pay a tribute to Sun Wen, as he was affectionately known, and made a pilgrimage to the Temple of the Azure Clouds. I climbed the steep marble stairs, passing terrace after terrace to the topmost level. There, in a square room, was the coffin of the liberator of the people, surrounded by displays of paper flowers. Outside the doorway stood a single youthful soldier in a gray, baggy, cotton uniform with a rifle in his hand. He was the only honor guard. I was the only visitor.

Nearly five years passed before Dr. Sun's remains were removed to Nanjing and placed in the National Mausoleum on Purple Mountain.

A few weeks after Sun's funeral Sue and I were guests in the home of Dr. H. H. Kung, who was a descendant of Confucius, a wealthy banker and a leader in the Guomindang. His wife was Ai-ling Soong, a sister of Ching-ling Soong, the wife of Dr. Sun and a sister of Mei-ling Soong, who married Chiang Kaishek. Dr. Kung was an Oberlin College graduate and was giving a party for the alumni in Beijing.

Talking with me about Sun Wen, he said, "His life was one long harrowing struggle, battling against the barriers that China presented to reform. He met a tidal wave of disappointments and reverses, sufficient to destroy an average man. But he remained a stubborn prophet who would not admit defeat. It is unfortunate that the democracies of the West, especially America, England and France, did not support him.

"It has been extremely difficult to engineer change in China without outside backing. The Russians offered advisers and funds. Sun was forced to look to the followers of Lenin. They were the only great power that offered tangible help. I wish that we might have been taken under the wing of my foster country, America, where we have many friends. But they waited too long."

Critics of Sun's stormy career mention that he lived abroad as an exile so many years that he lost touch with China's problems. Also they pointed out that he spent too much time with overseas Chinese and foreigners who knew little of developments in China. The reformer was a genius as a rebel against Manchu oppression but he was weak as an administrator.

However China owes a debt to Sun as an early liberator of the country from backwardness and stagnation. Christianity appealed to him as a liberating force and inspired him to oppose ignorance and superstition.

In August 1912 Sun spoke to Chinese Christians at the American Board Mission in Beijing: "Since the establishment of the Republic, the Chinese Church has not let an opportunity go by to show its loyal support of the new government.

"Men say that the revolution originated with me. I do not deny the charge. But where did the idea of the revolution come from? It came because from my youth I have had intercourse with foreign missionaries. Those Christians from Europe and America with whom I associated put the ideals of freedom and liberty into my heart. Now I call upon the church to help in the establishment of the new government. The republic cannot endure unless there is virtue - the righteousness for which the Christian religion stands at the center of the nation's life."[*]

Sun Wen praised the missionaries for their support of his Three Peopleism. They were out and out reformers. In their churches, schools, colleges, hospitals, social centers and agricultural projects they taught the illiterate to read and write, the impoverished to raise better crops and the sick to fight disease. Mao Tzdong refused to recognize the fact that the missionaries he despised and exiled had undermined the Ching tyranny and blazed trails toward emancipation.

Mao's record of abuses of Christian educators, clergy, doctors of medicine, business people and scientists struck a suicidal blow at the welfare of the country, destroying outstanding leaders and impoverishing the nation. These inquisitions along with the orgies of the Cultural Revolution set China back half a century.

Christian missionaries from western countries paid a price for their uninvited presence when the Communists came to power. The Party launched an open war against religion as the "opium of the

---

[*] Lyon Sharman

people." Most of the missionaries were exiled from the country. Some were persecuted and imprisoned. Their churches, schools, hospital and social service centers were seized and their leaders forced to flee for their lives.

Liang Qichao

Liang Qichao
Dean of the Reformers

LIANG QICHAO WAS THE SON and grandson of classical scholars. At age eleven he won the title of *sheng yuan* (a licentiate of the first degree). He studied and taught in the academy of the famous reformer, Kang Yuwei and worked with him in many progressive causes. Confronted with arrest, Liang took refuge in the Japanese Embassy. He studied in Japan where he was involved in reform movements to topple the Manchu government. He was threatened by the Empress Dowager and Yuan Shikai who plotted to assume the role of emperor.

He was my neighbor while he taught at Tsing Hua University, next door to my home at Yenching University. His name was a byword in the academic world. For long years he had pioneered as a liberator of the people, lecturing, writing and working for a constitutional, democratic government. He welcomed me as a youthful writer who shared his world views.

While clinging to his Confucian heritage and his Buddhist faith, he advocated rebuilding on the old foundations. He urged his country to learn from the technology and science of the West. He had traveled widely in Europe, America and Asia on government missions.

One of the first movements he founded was called Renovation of the People and he signed his name "a renovated man." In his magazine, *The New People,* he wrote in *pai hua,* the vernacular of the people, not in *wen li*, the classical language of scholars. *The New People* was concerned about the stagnant and backward state of China, the dominance of despots and war lords. It was incumbent upon the people to be informed and active in politics.

Liang was back of countless good causes, founding an anti-foot binding society and advocating the rights of women. He and his wife organized a school for the education of girls. He urged citizens to devote themselves to service of society during China's struggles for survival.

He was depressed by his travels in Europe following World War I, by the chauvinistic nationalism that led to continual wars. He spoke against the materialism of the West and the indifference toward spiritual values. "Western Europe has blindly followed the dark shadow of science and has been led away from spiritual values that shape human judgment. Materialism is not the key to everything. Many Europeans are adrift, sunk in doubt, depression and fear, due to nationalism and adulation of science."

He participated in the World Conference of Buddhists in 1923, speaking out against the anti-religious movements. For him Buddhism represented the path of faith through enlightenment of the mind, the achievement of perfection through one's own efforts. He commended much in Confucian ethics as the basis for character in family and state.

During a visit with Dr. Liang two years before his death he spoke of his anxiety over China's infatuation with Communist Russian advisers who were infiltrating the country. "I am opposed to Karl Marx," he said. "I do not believe that class struggle can bring progress to society. There is no such absolute as class entity since classes are mobile and always changing. The economic interpretation of history is unacceptable. The materialism of Marx and Lenin is not what this country needs.

"There are different kinds of imperialism. The imperialism of the Soviet Union is the crystal form. Karl Marx is the god of the pantheon and Lenin is Peter the Great. Soviet panaceas are not right for China. They are alien to Chinese culture. The materialistic dialectic, class hatred and violent revolution are foreign to my people. If we continue to be deceived we will face tragedy."

My host spoke with the composure of a scholar who had delved deep into the verities of Chinese wisdom. He had founded the Comparative Study Society to translate significant books of the West and the *Philosophie Magazine* to interpret Chinese and western philosophy.

He lectured widely during his last years at the following universities: Nankai, Tungan, Tsinghua, Yenching and the National University. He was welcomed as the scholar statesman who presented a philosophy above the level of current cynicism and Marxist materialism.

The spring of 1927 was a period of acute tension due to the breakdown between the Guomindang and the Communist Party and there were widespread anti-foreign movements. On March 30 Dr. Liang wrote his two sons, who were studying in America, one at the University of Pennsylvania and one at Cornell:

"Though we now have absolutely clear evidence that Chiang Kaishek and his people are not Communists, I fear that not even they themselves dare say whether or not they will have the capabilities of controlling the Communists. Shanghai at present is the prey being struggled over by both parties. It is an incredibly desperate situation. If the Communists emerge as the victors, then the rest of us won't even know what our final fate will be. Beijing itself is like an enormous powder keg, just waiting for something to set it off."*

Following the killings of Westerners in Nanjing we were told by the embassy in Beijing to be ready to leave the country in twelve hours.

In 1929 Liang Qichao who had championed the cause of reform for decades, passed away at Beijing Union Medical College.

* Jonathan D. Spence

Lu Xun

Lu Xun
Satirist of China

HERE I WAS IN THE HOME of Lu Xun, the Chekov of China. His barbed and challenging stories made him the idol of the young revolutionaries. One of my students was his ardent admirer and arranged the visit with the novelist.

Lu Xun was known by his *nom de plume* and seldom made use of his true name, Chou Shujen. In his mid-forties he was sturdy and self-confident with short, bristly moustache and close-cropped hair. He strode back and forth behind his desk in his blue robe and black cloth shoes. His manner was brusque and his answers to questions incisive.

Lu Xun had studied medicine in Japan where he was introduced to Chinese revolutionaries who were planning the overthrow of the Manchu dynasty. He discovered that his pen could work for that cause. He urged writers "to laugh, to weep, curse and to strike. Too many are content to paint rosey pictures in the midst of chaos. Writers lack the courage to face reality, coyly welcoming the magpie (symbol of good luck) while shunning the owl (symbol of the ominous)."

Lu Xun was a radical, stubbornly independent and always critical. He said to me, "Confucianism and Buddhism are dead and can never revive. I do not believe in God. Morality and science are sufficient for modern man. The Chinese people are not religious and will never be. The trouble with the Chinese is that they are lazy. When they go to work civil war and disorder will cease and China

85

will no longer be sick. Work and science are her salvation."

In stark and biting style he laid open the malignant infections in Chinese society, challenging his people to wake up and abolish the superstitions and lethargy that blighted the land. He rebuked adulation of the past such as writing in the classical formalism instead of using *pai hua*, the vernacular tongue. He demanded equal rights for women and denounced the hokus pocus of superstition that flourished in China. "Let the weak cling to the past. The earth today should be inhabited only by people with a firm hold on the present. We have two choices - to embrace the ancient literature and die or forsake the ancient literature and live."

Lu Xun knew from his boyhood the hardships of the peasants, "who are overwhelmed by too many sons, famine, oppressive taxes, officials and gentry until they become wooden images. China must learn that there is more to the world than the Celestial Kingdom. The masses must open their minds to the West. Today the country is a black vat of human flesh, corrupt and weakened."

Picking up a translation of Charles Darwin, he said, "China must waken from her long sleep and welcome new technologies and concepts. They are not foes of China. Here is a box of matches which brings fire making within the reach of every man. It is a handy tool with which to light a fire on a wintry night. But, of course, with the same match a man may light a bomb. The scientific discoveries of the West, properly applied to the needs of China, will bring us progress."

Lu Xun sympathized with some Communist objectives because of his resentment of social evils, economic injustices, foreign intervention and the ineptitudes of Guomindang leaders. He was threatened with arrest by the Nationalist Government because of his criticism of the Guomindang but his popularity with the people protected him.

He shied away from the dogmas of Marx and Lenin. The Russian novelists were his favorites and he translated many of them but he never read the writings of Lenin or Marx's *Das Kapital*.

While teaching at Amoy University and Sun Yatsen University in Canton he engaged in bitter arguments with the Communists, at the same time urging reform among the Guomindang. The conflict between the military forces of Mao and Chiang troubled him deeply.

Sometime after the death of Lu Xun in 1936 the People's Republic built a memorial in his honor. Chairman Mao hailed him "Lu Xun the Communist, the giant of China's Revolution."

Mao recognized that Lu Xun was the voice of the people and wanted to claim him as a follower.

Lu Xun's brother, Dr. Chou Tsojen, who served as professor of Chinese philosophy at Yenching University, where I sometimes visited with him, denied that his brother had ever supported Marx and Lenin.

Li Dazhao, photograph taken by the author a few hours before Li's capture and sentence to death.

Li Dazhao
Founder of Chinese Communism

I WAS THE LAST WESTERN writer to interview Li Dazhao in the Soviet Embassy in Beijing before his capture and execution. Li was one of the popular figures at the Beijing National University. He was the driving force in China's Communist revolution.

Every time a war lord took over the capital the literati revolutionists had to go into hiding or exile. Beijing was captured three times during our residence there from 1924 - 1927, after frantic warnings of carnage and looting as the hostile troops encircled the walls. We never knew the number of casualties but we realized there had been a change of control when we saw human heads hanging in bamboo cages from the street light posts.

Most feared of all was General Zhang Zuolin of Manchuria who pushed south, with the aid of the Japanese, to take over Beijing in 1927. He was a hunter of liberals, especially Communists, and ordered the arrest of Professor Li, who took refuge with his family in the Soviet Embassy.

Li was an orphan of a peasant family. Graduating from the Peiyang School of Law and Government, he plunged into work for the revolution. After further studies in Japan he wrote critically of the flaws in his country - the pessimistic outlook, lethargy, fatalistic dependence on the gods, lack of initiative and suppression of women.

In 1918 he was invited to serve as librarian of the National University. He was welcomed into the distinguished company of scholars who were spearheading the revolution. Li had been delving deep into Karl Marx and published *The Victory of Bolshevism*. "We are caught up in a redemptive movement," he wrote, "in that it cannot be halted by capitalist countries. Emperors, bureaucrats and warlords will be destroyed as by a thunderbolt."

Mao Tzdong, the young back country peasant, was given a job in the library at eight dollars a month, where he joined Li's seminar, the Red Chamber. He was taught to go to the country and the factories and enlist the peasants and workers.

Li Dazhao founded the Communist Party of Beijing and his associate, Chen Duxiu, founded the Communist Party of Shanghai. Li was called "the friend of everyone," finding jobs for students and giving them loans.

When I met Dr. Li he looked to me like a kindly professor in his long brown robe, black shoes and heavy bone eyeglasses. He was somewhat stocky at 48, with a droopy dark moustache and was tense from his life of confinement. Speaking excellent English, he said, "I have sought refuge in strange spots, sometimes in the home of a friend and often in a Buddhist temple and in the mountains. Recent years have been distressing. Efforts at reform have been checked by weak government and by the warlords."

My host leaned forward from his straight chair. "I am a disciple of Marx and Lenin. China's need is a complete revolution. I accept the economic interpretation of history. The Chinese are unreligious and practical."

His voice was rising and he struggled to put into words deep emotional adulation for his revolution.

"I came to my decision after long years of probing," he continued. "There is no other way to help my people. As the masses are organized we will feel an irresistible thrust and will join comrades in Russia and other countries in the inevitable victory of Communism."

I could sense in Li the mystic infatuation that characterized some of my students. They had found the wave of the future. There was a Messianic commitment to the golden age that was dawning.

My host had ventured forth from his library to engage in a few demonstrations but he had never participated in violent revolution. This idealist who had labored with Liang Qichao and Hu Shi and other democratic pioneers was ensnared by the dream of the new age under Marx and Lenin.

With his arm in mine, the professor led me into the office of the Soviet ambassador to China, Leo M. Karajhan, who extended a hand and in a booming voice said, "We are the new missionaries of a new age in China. We offer the people rice, not pious dogma. The Christian missionary era is gone forever. We are here to stay. Our mission is to save China through a gospel that will surpass any so-called miracle that was ever wrought by the cross and holy relics."

On April 7, 1927, Marshal Zhang Zuolin's troops raided the Soviet Embassy and arrested Li Dazhao. He was sentenced to death and was strangled three weeks later on April 28. His remains were hidden in a Buddhist temple to prevent demonstrations.

Professor Li, the book convert to Marxism, discovered a genius in his student, Mao Tzdong. The penniless peasant was Li's favorite in the Red Chamber Club. Under Li's tutelage, in twenty-two years this protègè became the Party Chairman of the largest Communist country in the world.

Hu Hsi

Hu Shi
Champion of Western Knowledge

I HAD HEARD ABOUT Hu Shi in my study of the Chinese Revolution at Yale. He set out in 1910 with a Boxer Indemnity Scholarship for study in America. Seven years later, with a B.A. degree and a Phi Beta Kappa key from Cornell and a Ph.D. from Columbia, he returned to Beijing to serve as professor of Chinese and Western Philosophy at the National University. He was twenty-six years old.

The young scholar's mother was pleased by his achievements. She was his father's third wife, married when she was sixteen. Hu Shi was her only child. After the death of her husband she exhibited skill in keeping the family together, handling the step children and paying the bills. Conscious of the bright mind of her son, she sacrificed to provide him with a tutor in the classics at an early age. Throughout her life he praised the guidance his mother had provided. She arranged for his engagement to a local girl, whom he married after his return from America.

"When it comes to family, I will stay with Chinese tradition. When it comes to politics I look to the West," he said to me in his office at the National University, surrounded with his library of Chinese and Western philosophy. He was slender in build, of modest height, a dynamo of energy, a fluent and eloquent speaker.

He criticized the inertia and standardization created by Confucian ethics. He admired Hendrik Ibsen and translated his plays to wake up his people. "Renaissance means a new attitude. We ask questions about traditional customs. Are they justifying their existence? Are the ideas of the ancient sages correct for today? If a principle is no longer useful, exchange it."

Hu was a force in the Intellectual Renaissance. His motto was "a radical re-evaluation of everything." He started with the language, urging writers to use *pai hua*, the vernacular of the common people instead of the stilted classical style. "No dead language can produce a living literature. Don't imitate the ancients. Don't use high sounding words. Don't indulge in saying nothing."

He spoke of his studies with John Dewey at Columbia and liked his concern for society rather than with religion. He took over Dewey's method of historical criticism.

He said he disagreed with the Marxist, Li Dazhao, who argued that China must go through a sweeping violent revolution like Russia. "We have plenty of revolution surging about us in China," he pointed out. Nothing constructive could be added through violence. He was devoted to his mentors, Charles Darwin, Thomas Huxley, Hendrik Ibsen, John Dewey and Bertrand Russell.

He was a rationalist and a realist. Hu said, "It is better to trust man than to trust Heaven. It is better to depend upon one's self than to depend upon God. We are not waiting for the future Kingdom of Heaven, but we are building a peaceful human society on the earth. We are not thinking wildly about living an immortal life as an angel; we want to be active and healthy men. We are not so credulous as to believe that God is almighty, but we believe that the scientific method is almighty and the future of mankind is unlimited. We are not going to believe any more in the immortality of the soul, but rather that personality and human rights are sacred and holy.

"It is true that the East has religions which advocate universal love, but it is only in the West that freedom, equality and fraternity have been carried out in practice. The collapse of the old class system, overthrow of despotic governments, the concept of equality before the law, the freedom of belief, thought and speech, and publication, the spread of education, the liberation of women, all these are manifestations of the new religion and morality of the West."

As one who placed his faith in science and the empirical method Hu disagreed with Liang Qichao, the Buddhist, and Liang Shuming, the Confucianist, who emphasized the materialism of the West and the superior spiritual qualities of the Orient.

Hu wrote: "Modern western civilization by no means disregards the spiritual needs of mankind. It is able to satisfy the needs of man's mind and spirit to a degree far surpassing anything the older eastern civilization could ever dream of. With the East there is quiet acceptance of one's appointed lot, with poverty, desire to please Heaven, non-resistance and endurance of misery. In the West there is dissatisfaction with one's appointed lot, with poverty, with willingness to endure misery."

In one of our conversations Dr. Hu mentioned that he studied the Christian religion while he was a student at Cornell and almost accepted it as his faith. But his rational nature and his heritage said no. His keen mind pointed out the flaws in the Christian Missionary Enterprise in his frank and pithy style.

"Christianity in China is a foreign enterprise, originated in an alien culture and appears to Chinese as a form of religious imperialism. Exponents of numerous Christian sects pushed their way in within the wake of the Opium Wars and the Boxer Expeditionary troops, under the protection of foreign concessions and gun boats. Too many of these missionaries are outsiders who are ignorant of China's culture, ethics and religion. They berate deference toward Chinese sages while they glorify Jesus, Paul, Augustine, Calvin and Luther.

"They scorn values that have created and sustained the Chinese for 3,000 years and attempt to impose a western way of life. The churches they build are not Chinese in appearance, but are copies of Saxon, Gothic, Roman or American styles. Discarding respect for Chinese ancestors, they set up their own pantheon of heroes. They condemn the tablets found in Confucian temples and then place a cross on their altars. They ridicule Buddhist statues, but defend stations of the cross, pictures of Jesus and the saints."

Hu continued with a smile, "Chinese intellectuals do not want to affiliate with the North China Branch of the Methodist Church South. It sounds like a railroad station rather than a religious institution, and of course it carries a name utterly foreign to China."

In July, 1937, while he was absent from Beijing participating in conferences on the national emergency, the Japanese attacked the capital, and soon controlled Shanghai and Nanjing. Declaring his support of the Nationalist government, Hu set out for America and Europe to interpret the cause of his people. He was to remain abroad for eight years since he was appointed Chinese ambassador to the United States. He returned to China in 1946 to act as chancellor of the Peking National University.

In 1950, after the Communists were in power, Party henchmen employed their character assassination technique on Dr. Hu's son, Dr. Hushidu. He was forced to issue a public denunciation of his father that was circulated throughout the republic. The denigration contained all the derogatory words employed by the Party. The blast of vituperation was followed by symposia throughout the republic where the Senior Hu's record was condemned.

With the Maoist occupation of Beijing Dr. Hu had flown to America to lecture at Princeton and other universities. In 1958 he moved to Taiwan to serve as president of the Academia Sinica. Following a public reception there on February 24, 1962, he died from a heart attack.

His passing saved him further harassment at the hands of the Maoists who were soon to launch that orgy of libel and defamation called the Cultural Revolution. Even after his demise he was considered a sinister foe of Communism. Party inquisitors continued their fulminations against his books and his popularity with the people.

Dr. Hu Shi had said, "Under Communism you do not have even the freedom of silence."

Part III
New China

A Gentleman of New Beijing

Gliding through Tien An Men Square,
Speeding along broad Hatamen Boulevard,
The gleaming black limousine
Carries a new gentleman
Serene in woolen topcoat
Lined with choicest beaver pelts.
The cotton uniform worn in
The caves of Yanan was discarded
When he moved into Beijing
With the victorious conquerors.

The natty chauffeur, confident because
Of the prestige of his passenger,
Honks brazenly at the pedicabs and
Weaves in among the bicycles
Of the workers of a lesser rank
Who gaze with awe at the exalted
Commissar who had made his way
Into the higher echelon
To the inner circle who
Control the lives of one billion people.

The gentleman on the way to
His walled-in villa in the Western Hills
Tips his beaver hat over his eyes
And closes his mind to the harassments
Of the day: jealousies, intrigues and
The bunglings of a vast bureaucracy.
Soon his servants would prepare
Those cherished Canton dishes
And he would enjoy
Wines from his cellar
And the pleasures of his new wife,
A modern beauty from the south.

He had journeyed far
Since the Long March and the War of Liberation.

The New Morality

Chairman Mao says No
To the Five Relations
Upheld by countless generations:
The relation between prince and minister
The relation between father and son
The relation between elder brother and younger
Brother
The relation between husband and wife
The relation between friend and friend.

Chairman Mao says Yes
To the Five Loves:
Love for the fatherland
Love for the people
Love for labor
Love for science
Love for public property
Long live Chairman Mao!

The Walls Came Tumbling Down

Soon after Mao was proclaimed Chairman
    Of the People's Republic in
October 1949 he struck a blow at the
    Establishment. He ordered the demolition
Of the majestic walls of Beijing. It was a
    Repudiation of Confucian culture
In keeping with his motto, "Destroy the
    Old. Build the new."

The walls of the inner Tarter City had
    Been erected by Kublai Khan in the
Tenth century. The Mings built the massive
    City walls between 1421 and 1439.
They were as wide as a city street
    with castle-like towers
Rising sixty feet. Foreigners were granted
    The privilege of walking on this
Elevated stone highway from which they
    Could look out through openings in
The parapets on a view of the capital and
    The Forbidden City.

The walls were more than a medieval defense.
	They symbolized the spiritual values
Preserved for centuries in the Eternal City
	Where the Son of Heaven ruled under a
System of cosmic geometry that kept him and
	His people in harmony with the order of
The universe. The Herculean wrecking plans
	Were initiated in 1950 and continued for
Twelve years. The dust and din of the
	Operation haunted the capital
Like a funeral pall. Thousands
	Toiled to wipe out the past.

It was a shock to troubled citizens who
	Wondered what the Proletariat Revolution
Would demolish next. They shook their heads
	At this waste and violation of landmarks
Of generations and at such cost.

In the midst of this destructivity planners
	Of a modern socialized Beijing sacrificed
Handsome *pailous* and archways which had
	Brought touches of beauty with their
Shades of blue, green, red and gold. They
	Removed many "reactionary relics."[*]

---

[*] Simon Leys

Liang Ssuch'eng, the prominent architect,
    Lifted his voice in defense
Of these works of art, protesting against
    The plan to strip Beijing
Of her treasures. The Maoist authorities
    Confronted architect Liang, accusing him
Of being a "reactionary and a running dog of
    Western imperialism." He was compelled
To silence his protest and to publicly
    Condemn his illustrious father,
Dean of the Chinese revolutionaries,
    Liang Qichao.

This Was My Land

This was my land,
The good earth held by
My ancestors and nurtured by
Their toll for generations.
Today it lies within the boundaries
Of the Glorious Revolution Commune.

Tractors have displaced my faithful ox,
Now all is sorghum and soy beans
Where once grew my turnips and cabbage.
The gray brick cottage where my sons were born
Is now a store house.
It is better to share the land, they say,
To dwell together and
Eat in the great hall,
Where one can constantly be enlightened
By broadcasts, self-criticism, struggle meetings
And quotations from the Great Helmsman
Who brought us our freedom.
There is now one father for all the land.

But I steal away from the raucous radio
And sit alone, looking down at my old home.
I like to remember it as it was,
Welcoming smoke from the chimney
As I tramped in from my field,
Pigs, chickens, children and
The warmth of my kitchen with the
Smell of bread cakes on the stove -
But that was before, long ago,
And must be forgotten.

The loud speaker sounds forth
Its shrill call for the evening lecture.
I turn my steps back.
There is no time for remembering the past.
There is no place for a reactionary today.

Farewell, Confucius

Stripped of its dignity and grace,
The temple of Confucius stands forlorn,
Deserted by the sons of Han.
One sees within the dim interior
The ancient altar and the tablets
To the master and his disciples,
Now dust-blown and in disarray.

Bats sweep among the pillars
And skim the ceiling emblazoned
With symbols of the old learning.
Upon the tile floor, where reverent feet
Once stood, there rest a steam roller,
Wheel barrows, road tools
And a huge platform used for mass
Gatherings in the court yard, along with
Benches, amplifiers and portraits of Mao
For the education of the people in
The ways of the Revolution.
On the birthday of the sage and at the new year
The venerable shrine is closed and padlocked.
No longer do seekers come
To meditate upon the wisdom
Of the fathers or seek the will of Heaven.

For centuries they crowded the courtyard,
Set in a grove of cedar and ginko, striving to
Learn of *Li* and *Jen*,
Virtues left behind in the
Onward march of liberated men.

The hoo poe sounds his pensive call,
A chill wind blows an eddy of sand
Against the weather-beaten door
As the mantle of night enfolds
This memorial to the mentor of 2,500 years.

(*Li* - manners; *Jen* - benevolence)

Deification of the Man
of the Hour

Guo Moruo, poet laureate of the Chinese
Communist Party, was eloquent in his adulation
of Chairman Mao. While he was president of
the Chinese Academy of Science he wrote:

"During an international forum in Beijing
Mao Tzdong received
Some of the participants
And gave one of them his hand.
The fortunate man shared his delight
With his colleagues who
Advised him to bathe his hand
In a large basin
So that the others, too, could rinse their
Hands in the same water."*

The cult of Mao was promoted by teaching
the peasants to chant words of praise like the
Mountain Climbing Song from Inner Mongolia:

---

* George Urban

"We worship no god, nor temples build,
Chairman Mao's love is greater still.
Gods we destroy and temples tear down,
Better than gods we worship One Man.
Mountains may shake, earth may quake
And we are not afraid.
But we dare not forget
What the Chairman said."*

---

* Roderick MacFarquar

The Red Guard

The thunder of trampling feet,
The shouts of revolt and rage,
Seas of harsh young faces,
Banners waving, slogans flung into the air.
They shatter the tranquility.
Citizens scurry within their gates.
Shop keepers frantically man their shutters
And the ancient city braves itself
For another ordeal of human passion.

They surge in like rabble hoards before them:
Manchus, Boxers, western soldiers,
War lords, Japanese, the People's Army,
To disturb the cherished peace that comes
In moments of security. Now the Red Guard
Declaim against all things old,
Old culture, old ideas,
Old customs, old habits.

They "speak bitter" against the foundation
Of the past, hurling vituperation
At disciples of the sages.
The timeless capital trembles
Before their raging violence.

Released from school and all restraints,
They crowd the trains and roadways everywhere,
Venting their resentment against scholars, officials,
Merchants, housekeepers, all who might
Impede their efforts to recapture
The revolutionary zeal
And compel all to conform.

They invade the privacy of citizens
And strip their homes of bourgeois furnishings;
They accost parents, uncles, aunts and cousins
And condemn them for reactionary attitudes;
They beat police and magistrates
Until they confess their errors and immoralities;
And hang teachers and officials
Who are judged to be out of line
With Red Guard standards of the Revolution.
They burn books and desecrate temples.
They cry, "Everybody criticize everybody!
Away with the reactionaries!
Down with the land lords!
Down with the imperialists!
Up with the People's Republic !"

No Flowers in the Hair

No more roses in the hair,
No doggies to pet,
No bowl of goldfish on the kitchen table.
Bird songs must go to conserve the grain.
Bourgeoisie flowers were uprooted.
No place for beauty.
Conform. Dress alike in gray.
Think Party thoughts.
The new era of realism had arrived.
Temples became warehouses.
The materialism of Mao prevailed.

Yang and Yin

The universe, so the sages taught, is
Half *yang* and half *yin*,
Positive and negative,
Male and female.
They are forever in contention,
Back and forth.
When *yang* prevails
Peace and plenty;
When *yin* leads
Turmoil and trouble.

Man is a product of *yang*,
Woman is a child *yin*.
Hence Heaven has willed
That man should rule
His subject, the weaker half,
Who shall be subordinate.
In spite of the *yin* thesis t ere has
Been a disconcerting procession of female
Celebrities disturbing the annals
Of the Middle Kingdom
From Yang Kuei Fei
To the Empress Dowager Tz'u Hsi,
Concubines, dancers, artists, poets,
From the mother of Mencius
To Chairman Mao's Jiang Qin.

Yin appears to have
Set things at sevens and eights.
In New China it keeps one busy guessing
Who is *yang* and who is *yin*
With everyone camouflaged
In gray and blue jackets and trousers,
With short hair,
All commixed and commingled,
While planting rice, driving tractors,
Managing factories, performing surgery.
And this may be the reason why
The Great Leap Forward failed:
Yin, on the move
Was too much for *yang*.

No Thanks, Christians

A Chinese seeker set forth to
Observe the Christian way.
The Roman Catholic Church offered him
A trinity of deities plus a virgin goddess,
The Latin tongue,
Infallible law from the Vatican,
A variety of relics and superstitions,
The miracle of the mass.

The Anglicans presented
A Saxon style edifice,
A Prayer Book and Articles
In Elizabethan English,
An immaculate conception and
Resurrection of the body,
A hymnal without a note of Oriental music.

The Presbyterians
Boasted a solid replica of
An Akron Plan ecclesiastical plant,
Barren of the grace of a Confucian shrine,
Ample dogma and Genevan restraints,
And the assurance that John Calvin
Would replace the sages of Asia.

They all appeared to his Chinese mind
As foreign enterprises divorced from
The faith, ethics and culture of Cathay,
All promoters of an alien way.
The religious invasion of his homeland
Brought a confusion of
High churchmen and Pentecostals,
Purveyors of white civilization,
One sect against another sect,
Aggressive intruders who came uninvited,
Intent on proselyting their pagan host.

To clear his perplexity
The seeker left these
Christian compounds,
Little islands of extraterritoriality,
And made his way to the Temple of Heaven,
Where 3,000 years before
The emperor worshipped one invisible god,
The spirit of Heaven, on
Behalf of his nation.

Why should he turn from their truth
And follow after strange Caucasians
From outside the bounds of
The Celestial Kingdom?

The Golden Mean

The grace of Chinese womanhood and
The gentility of the sage
Delivered deft blows at the
Dialectical Materialism of Karl Marx
Their natural wisdom demanded
The return of roses to the hair,
Glistening goldfish,
Dogs wagging their tails
And birds warbling once again.

The Way is Not in Strife

In written stone the wise refrain
Tells of time and will remain
To point amid forlorn decay
Back centuries to a learned way
When princes sought with zealous care
To give to all a rightful share
And stole away to mountain nooks
To search for truth in sacred books.

Many years have crept and sped
Since his scholarly group by Laotzu was led.
Here I perceive the truth of his life,
The Way of Heaven is not in strife.
The characters once fresh on the white marble slab
Have been blown by the dust and washed into drab
While nature's cruel force and man's blinded
Reason
Proclaim it as folly and name it as treason.

The courtyard is ruined and the shrine has no
Cover.
No worshippers now, only birds as they hover.
The priests have all gone. There is no ritual or
Beauty,
Only the military pacing off duty.
Tents under the cedars, gun clanks on the floor,
Side arms stacked by the unhinged temple door.

A bugle sounds nightfall and they march off to rest.
One stands at the stone below a blue magpie's nest
To ponder these words that formed his golden
Mean,
Repudiate strife; seek inner peace serene.

(Written at a temple before a stone inscription in honor of
Lao-tzu.)

The Ching Ming Festival

Rebuked by the chill winds
    From the Gobi Desert, one morning
The bleak, dust-blown imperial
    City will be cheered
By scattered pear and peach
    Blossoms, peering over the brick walls of
Courtyards, like bright faces in the drab
    Monotone of dying winter.

Crocuses will add their gold and purple
    And song sparrows will trill their
Salute to the morning sun. Willows
    Will drop their graceful boughs
Against the towering city wall.

With the rebirth of nature, people think of
    Ching Ming, the time set aside for
Remembering their ancestors. They make
    Pilgrimages to the countless resting
Places of their forebears. They sweep away
    The dust and leaves and place
Flowers on the graves.

The bond of the family created century-old
　　Ties between the living and the dead.
Elaborate preparations are planned to
　　Guide the spirit of the deceased.
The body is borne in a great catafalque
　　To the grave.　The mourners dress in
White.　They scatter money along
　　The way to provide care for the
Departed.　They leave gifts of food and wine.

A people without memory are soon
　　Impoverished.　A people who respect
Their predecessors add to their
　　Wisdom and happiness.

A Mild Thaw

People were perplexed
About the Liberation of 1949. They
Were frightened by the glaring portraits
Of Engels, Marx and Lenin
That accompanied Chairman Mao.
Emblazoned across the land
Were admonitions, "Down with compradore
Culture," "Away with capitalist
Roaders" and "Down with running dogs of
Imperialism." Everything belonged
To the Party. No more private business,
No stands, tea-houses or restaurants
Along the streets.

Beijing assumed a drabness that might
Have been inflicted by a natural calamity.
People were ordered to work at becoming
Socialized. To *War-i-war* (strolling
And shop looking) was forbidden. No more
Enjoyment of bargaining. The pageantry
Of venders was halted.

No more candymen, persimmon peddlers
And apple carts; no charcoal salesmen, beating
Drums; no baked sweet potatoes or roasted
Chestnuts, tantalizing one's nostrils; no
White mice showman with his bugle. All such
Activities were "coattails of capitalism."

The drama of Beijing life had jolted to a
Discordant halt under the Marxist-Leninist
Regimentation. The monotone
Was like the blue-gray
Uniforms with men, women and children
Dressing alike and
Thinking alike.

But Deng Xiaoping, who had been disgraced
And persecuted by Mao, spoke critically
Of the Helmsman
Soon after he was laid to rest in
His mausoleum. Although a Communist,
Deng reaffirmed the pragmatic heritage that a
Theory is sound if it produces results.
He said that propaganda
Should be abandoned and
Production encouraged.
"A black cat, a white cat - it is a good
Cat if it catches mice."[1]

The economic reforms of Deng encouraged
People to "get rich quick" through engaging in
Private enterprise.
The commune extravaganza
Was replaced by moves to lease
Land to farmers
Who would cultivate it
And keep all profits
Above their rental, which was paid in produce.

---

[1] Harrison Salisbury

Many have built their own
homes on the land.

Billboards advertised coveted articles
Like radios, televisions,
Washing machines and
The latest car models. The free
Market concept set in motion an
Outpouring of energy
That had been restrained
By Party dogma. Peasants produced
Excess crops which they sold on
The free market.

Food venders returned along with tea
Stands, restaurants and inns. The hawkers
Appeared with their carts, jovial and
Articulate, up and down the *hutungs*
Projecting their summons to buy
Into the Soviet-style
Apartment complexes and over walls
Into courtyards. Small booths
Sprang up. Salesmen
Spread their wares along the streets,
Clothing, hats, shoes, jewelry, wood crafts
And pottery. These coat-tail entrepreneurs
Were again part of the hustle of Beijing.[1]

---

[1] Orville Shell

The Family -- China's Most Enduring Contribution

The Middle Kingdom has set many records.
It invented gun powder, paper, porcelain, the
Compass, silk cloth,
And most significant of all
The family system that has survived for
3,000 years.

There were others before Confucius who
Gathered the wisdom of the predecessors. An
Illustrious company of scholars followed him
Like Mencius, Lao Tzu and
Moti who built an
Enduring social structure. It has
Withstood cataclysmic change,
Including the assaults of
The first emperor, Ch'in Shih Huang
Who burned Confucian books and
Buried scholars alive
While he built his Great Wall
To the north and
His army of clay warriors
In his tomb in Xian.

Mao Tzdong followed a similar pattern.
He burned Confucian books and imprisoned
Scholars and ordered
The people to live in
Communes. In June 1956 it was
Reported that 108,000,000 families had
been "collectivised."
Mao urged the people "to work like ants
Removing a mountain" to reform
The family. He outlined rules
Against romantic love and the
Traditional customs.

"The relations between husbands and wives
Will be that they will live together
But eat separately
Because they may not work and study
Together. Although parents
Will not live together
All the year round they will see each
Other frequently. This could be called
A new family system.

But it is no longer a basic
Unit that organizes society. The family
Will not exist as a
Cell-forming unit."* However,
After nearly forty years, the family
Appears to be breaking up the communes.

---

* George Poloczi-Horvath

Spiritual concepts are embedded in the
Family practices that developed around birth,
Marriage and death.

One beautiful ritual centered
On the birth of a child.
Grandparents, uncles, aunts and cousins
Gathered. Small children dropped flower
Petals into the bath water and watched the
Ceremonial bathing of the baby.

The Chinese family built bridges between
Generations. Members demonstrated mutual aid
Through living together.
Team work helped
Maintain the home
And promote general welfare.
Elders contributed through sharing
Their experience and in teaching
Morality. Two or three generations
Together provided a social
Unit that gave security to the aged as well as
Enriching the minds of the young.
The sick and the old
Were cared for by their
Children and relatives.

A Continuing Heritage

The humblest factory worker and peasant
Farmer look with respect
Upon the written language
Of their ancestors. How this
Overpowering complexity
Of hieroglyphics came into being
Is a tribute to the skill of the
Antiquarians who experimented with brush and
Ink for centuries
To perfect *Wen Li,* the
Classical language of the elite.

Tang, Ming and Ching emperors were glad
To keep this brain trust of the
Country totally engrossed in academic
Pursuit of the inventory
Of thousands and thousands
Of varying characters. This
Preoccupation absorbed the energy
Of the scholars and kept
Them from creating a revolution.

The masses honored the scholars and the
Wisdom they represented.
They believed that a
Written character was sacred.

The four Chinese characters are (from top to bottom):

Jen for benevolence
I for justice
Ho Ping for peace

They dreamed of being
Able to read and write but through
Interminable dynasties of illiteracy ninety
Percent of the people
Remained chained in darkness.
In spite of their enslavement the
Illiterate honored learning.
The scholar was the top ranking member
Of society, above the official, the
Merchant and the soldier who
Stood at the bottom.

The classics written by the sages were
The foundation of education.
Children of tender age memorized
Passages from the wise men
Of antiquity. They learned early
That *Tien* was above the earth
And man in an empyrean realm
That preserved the order of the
Universe. Only when the emperor
And the sages led the people
In harmony with *Tien* could
There be peace and prosperity.
The superior man learned to live
In harmony with the long established
Precepts of *Tien*.

This outreach introduced man to *Li,*
The principle of order.
The state and the family
Were built on the orderly rites
Prescribed for man by *Tien.*
Man can be a part of this
Mannerly and cooperative living
Through exhibiting moral harmony
In his own life. *Li* meant
Social behavior where everything was in
Its place with people showing respect
For one another. *Li* was
The basis in human relations,
Good manners between child and parent,
All the way to prince and emperor.

Jen was another precept in the Chinese
heritage. *Jen* was benevolence,
The practice of consideration for others.
Confucius taught
"Do not do to others what you would
Not want others to do to you."
He believed in government by the
Intellectual class, government by
Example, the people being led by just
And compassionate men.

I, pronounced yee, meaning justice,
Is also a Confucian moral concept
Perhaps second only
To benevolence.

Ho and *ping* together express
The quality of peace,
A virtue emphasized in China's culture.

The characters by the calligrapher,
C. Y. Hsu, represent three
Of the most prized precepts
In Chinese philosophy:
Jen for benevolence,
I for justice and
Ho Ping for peace.

This ethical heritage has carried the
Chinese people through
Periods of confusion
And oppression. It is an inherited
And ingrained texture in Chinese character.
Chroniclers of the future may record
A renaissance of these traditions
Of 3,000 years.

The Call of the Phoenix

The phoenix is second only to the dragon in Chinese art and literature. This emperor of birddom is a favorite mythological figure, appearing in times of historic significance like the birth of Confucius. The phoenix is a special creation, more spectacular than the most royal of birds. Artists use a variety of colors to adorn the plumage with twelve resplendent tail feathers.

Werner's *Dictionary of Chinese Mythology* states that the phoenix is adorned with everything that is beautiful among birds. When it flies a train of small birds always attend it. Like the unicorn it is benevolent and will not peck or injure living insects or tread upon living herbs. It alights only upon the *wu t'ung* tree, feeds only on seeds of the bamboo and quenches its thirst only at the sweet fountains. It resides in the Vermillion Hills, where it eats and drinks at its pleasure, waiting for the time when peace shall pervade the country.

This divine bird, once recorded as being six feet in height, is often pictured gazing on a ball of fire. The sun being the *Yang*, or active principle, the phoenix has influence in the begetting of children.

Mr. C. Y. Hsu, a contemporary Sinolog, along with other scholars, speculates that the phoenix is not a myth but rather an extinct species. He says that many ancient Chinese writers claim to have seen it and describe it as a very colorful bird that called melodiously. Its first recorded appearance is in the reign of Huang Ti, the Yellow Emperor, in 2,500 B.C. It again showed itself in the next reign and two phoenixes nested in Yao's palace about 2,350 B.C.

It is not until the Han dynasty that we hear of worship being paid to it. Later its appearance becomes a commonplace in Chinese history and is seen to glorify a peaceful reign or flatter a successful ruler. There is a tradition that the phoenix appeared at the birth of Confucius. Although this is difficult to verify, Confucius did believe in the sacred bird. He wrote in his *Analects,* "The phoenix does not come and the river sends forth no diagrams. It is all over with me."*

The bird's last advent was at Feng-huang-fu in Anhwei, where it scratched at Hung Wu's father's grave, and the imperial power passed into Hung Wu's hands. (Hung Wu was the reign title of the first emperor of the Ming dynasty, Chu Yuan-chang, A.D. 1368-1399.)

With the blessing of the holy bird, the Ming dynasty endured from 1368 to 1644. The Ching dynasty came to power in 1644 and entered a tempestuous era in the late nineteenth century which culminated in Sun Yatsen's democratic revolt of 1911.

Contemporary observers who are confused by the tangled web of China's One Hundred Years of Revolution, might grasp this thread of hope that there will be a visit from the phoenix and the beginning of a new era of peace and freedom.

---

* Translated by C. Y. Hsu

A Chinese Farewell

再　　見

TSAI CHIEN